—— THE ——
Immigrant

THE
Immigrant

PETER ALBION

Order this book online at www.trafford.com
or email orders@trafford.com

Most Trafford titles are also available at major online book
retailers.

Printed in the United States of America.

ISBN: 978-1-4269-5504-4 (sc)
ISBN: 978-1-4269-5505-1 (e)

Library of Congress Control Number: 2011900194

Trafford rev.03/23/2011

 www.trafford.com

North America & International
toll-free: 1 888 232 4444 (USA & Canada)
phone: 250 383 6864 ♦ fax: 812 355 4082

peteralbion@atl.net,   408 504 5093   Peter M. Albion

CONTENTS

Prologue vii

Germany 1

Immigration 14

British Columbia 18

Why Capitalism Self-Destructs 21

In the Name of National Security 28

Is the Truth Hidden or Available? 31

Communism and Other Confusions 36

Self-Destruction in Disguise 42

What Does Sex Have to Do with It? 45

Are We Capable of Seeing the Big Picture 50

Can We Stop Believing? 56

Is Your Formless Self Stronger than Your Ego? ... 62

Belief Sleep 66

Nonresistance, the Strongest Power in the Universe .. 68

Dying for the Ultimate Illusion 71

Recommended Reading 75

Prologue

Travelers, shape shifters, actors of a kind? Fake it till you make it ,means as actors we are all practicing being present to our daily details, the actor knows when connection to space presents is in the play, he has made it. The diversity so complex, the play so perfect in its creation we forget, our birthright to Being. That which creates the macro and micro can't be known by the ego. Is your evolution, your waking up out of the dream of thought, guaranteed?

Civilizations have come and gone since Atlantis, possibly before, but humanity seems to make similar mistakes every time, destroying itself. What is this unconscious, destructive mechanism in the individual more dangerous in the collective? The atrocities committed by the collective are far greater than the ones committed by individuals.

In the name of national security, religion, superiority, race, and nationality, governments have killed more than one hundred million men, women, and children in the last century alone; we are the government. Who are those civil servants pushing for war every time, again and again and again? Why are they hiding behind the president and House and Senate? Special interest groups are only messengers—from whom?

Don't believe anything; begin the journey of knowing.

Formless being, space, silence, attention, present now, are words pointing to being. Observing without naming, participating without identification, be in this world but not of it, means you have made it, you are awake. Nobody reinforces your spirituality in your youth, speaks about your formless being self, who you really are. Special higher education made a contract with ego, form, and has forgotten your truth, Being!

When I left Germany, I said to my brothers, "Ask and you shall be given." It is a natural law, and I shall experience it.

To be or not to be—what is its truth?

I can say now, it is an instant answer in the present now, if I can be aware, silently present without identification of thoughts, pure awareness. That is Being, no answers can be found tomorrow. Be aware of your breathing, be alert, pay attention, be the observer and maintain ruthless honesty and seriousness with yourself; these are keys.

Germany

I was born in the agricultural region of East Germany. After 1945, East Germany was under Soviet control. It was supposedly a Communist state, but like its opposite, capitalism, it lacked humanistic, transparent, honest, uncorrupt, enlightened, nonviolent, united, loving leaders. Implementation of "all for one and one for all" was weak and, in the end, self-destructed, as any dogmatic system will self-destruct if it does not implement what is good for the whole, and for one, there is no separation. Capitalism is ego driven and on the path of self-destruction to this day.

My upbringing in East Germany was, from my perception looking back, life changing—not because of communism, but because of walls in people's hearts, identifications with form, pleasure, instant gratification, wanting more and more physical stuff. Where is Being in peoples life? Where is that meditative walk in nature, the silence, the looking without wanting, being where you are without complaining, being silently with your child, watching without telling what to do, or not. Being there with your nonresistant force guiding with your formless spirit, Love is in the detail.

So West Germany was created to satisfy this hunger for more stuff, yes, fancy stuff, if you like.

What you resist persists. What you fight you strengthen.

That is why communism failed; first, it is in its core the humanist system, capitalism, being more ruthless and ego driven uses all possible disguises to survive its self-destructive course, so it survives a little longer.

As a child and later as a young adult in East Germany, I had a good time at school, partially because the teachers loved their jobs. Yes, we had no Wall-mart, Play mart, Disney, shopping centers, and so on. But it was like heaven to go to the baker before school and buy fresh rolls for breakfast every morning; I loved the delicious smell of a poor bakery standing alone without cross-contaminated smells in a Safeway, or taking a simple walk in the forest picking mushrooms or playing in the creek or playing with marbles in the sand making something out of nothing as children. Unfortunately, that joy I had as a child was also educated out of me, by what we call the system of learning. Don't despair; it is still within you now.

When I was fourteen my grandfather Max arranged an apprenticeship for me as a butcher in a city close by, but far enough for me to feel abundant and alone in a new family. At the time, the apprenticeship included accommodations in the master's house and use of his living room. The master's daughter became my first love just before I was pulled out of that hard life.

Advertising in a Communist country was rather primitive compared to the bombardment of advertising in capitalistic West Germany, where I found myself when I was sixteen. I visited my parents' new business in West Germany in 1955. I had to take the train to Berlin and fly to Dusseldorf to visit. My recollection is that my mother was overcome by depression; I did not give her my love, which I did not realize I had within me. I said good-bye—no hug, no kiss, no looking into her eyes lovingly. What you don't have, you can't give. I did not feel the pain my mother was under, nor was I able to look into her eyes and feel a connection. I buffered the good-bye;, I was not present in the now, which is love. At the time that was on the other side of a mountain.

Six months earlier, Hilda, my grandfather's wife, had committed suicide in East Germany. That was my first big shock at fifteen years. *We actually die at some point?* How she died was even a bigger shock because of the religious stigma that was (and still is) attached to suicide. We, as a society, love to judge others. It is ego enhancing; the ego feels it is superior to others, by putting others down.

Grandfather and I were the only family at Hilda's funeral because the rest of the family, which was already in West Germany, was not able to come. The border was already closed for the return trip. So here was the church, judging my mother to be something evil and also judging me as her evil son. None of that was spoken, but in a religious family, the effect is confusion and depression.

Now I know that my mother helped me get off the religious path and onto the honest, spiritual way.

One of the big mistakes society, governments, or individuals make is to force people to do something they don't want to do. That is true for families as well. It always fails, sooner or later.

That physical wall splitting East and West Germany came down. But many have a wall within their heart, preventing them from being present to the simplicity of the wind brushing their cheek, looking and breathing without words; accepting without resistance is a way to be in the force of now.

Six months later, my mother committed suicide. The ego-driven world has no compassion, patience, or understanding of the formless self; it uses violence to shock insanity out of people. Force against force will create more pain. Only love can heal everything (not the physical kind of love).

That left only one woman in the family: my beloved grandmother Paula, my mother's mother. Paula was the one who gave me a spiritual grounding in my childhood; I only became aware of that much later.

The family fell apart after those two women were gone. Women are the spiritual glue of humanity; man destroys it. Another confusing element for me was the quick remarrying of my father. These early shocks and pains in my youth helped start the process of asking. Ask and you shall receive.

You don't know when answers will come at that stage. Youth, by its nature, is impatient; I tried to forget my youth, which I was successful in because I don't remember much around that time. Extreme identification and fear prevent one from being present; one is in a dream of thought state, disconnected from what is really happening around one.

After my mother's funeral, Grandfather went back to the East, and I stayed in Essen, West Germany, to help my father in his new business.

I discovered that I was an immigrant in my own country; East Germans were looked on as second-class citizens in West Germany. One does not have to go far to experience the weaknesses of humanity and feel the ego's indiscriminant ways of aggrandizement and justification.

Your family usually classifies you in a subtle way. Are you the firstborn, male, female, ego, intelligent, nerd, crippled in one way or another, and so on?

So I tried to get away from the family business. At the time I didn't know all the details, but I had a bad feeling about my parents. My mother suffered over my fathers philandering and his past. Self created enemies of my father created obstacles, they took his business away in East Germany and my older brother the first born was not allowed to become a butcher, among other discriminations and problems created by the local government against my family in essence against my father.

From the first observation, that looks unjust, but it has its roots in my father's youth, when he did something that followed him all his life. At the time, I did not know what was happening, but later he said to me that incident in his youth created problems for him and the family his whole life. The sins of the fathers and mothers revisit themselves onto the children for a long time, till the pain is used consciously.

Grandfather Max and I went to my mother's funeral in Essen; we were given visas, but we were told later that I was too young and Grandfather was too old. So I got out of the evil DDR; Grandfather went back because his life wasn't bad there, and you can't transplant an old tree. So I left behind the new family and my first love and everything else a sixteen-year-old accumulates and identifies with.

A mother's death is a shock to most. I erected an inner wall for many years. Capitalism helped to cover up the pain for a while, like a deception play. I did not want to go deep, did not want the truth through feeling the pain, consciously without resistance. I was resisting the truth.

Von Bremen to Halifax
Mid Atlantic, March 1965

Halifax — Vancouver BC

Space—Space—Space—Silence

Vancouver, Canada

Life—Nature—Love

Alta Lake Whisteler Mountain

Mount Robson

Rocky Mountains

Harvesting Grapes

Vinyard Oregon House

11

This was also only an excuse for my father's self-gratification, and deep down I probably was too liberal, not ruthlessly capitalistic. After all, I was his son, so he used me; it was his right, in his book.

So I helped in my father's business but made some good friends after work and on weekends, people who actually enjoyed life and their work, specifically in natural communication. I started to rediscover my inner self, not knowing it at the time. I enjoyed nature on weekends and after work. I discovered a strong attraction to a beautiful girl but had too many fears. I lived in the head, identifying with many complexes and imaginations, and at that time, I still believed as I was told. Belief was almost the strongest thought system I had to make transparent, to see what reality is: a physical thought that dies when the body dies. Belief is not who you are. I discovered that most of my friends at the time actually enjoyed life.

No one understood or had to go to the slaughterhouse and experience where the steak and sausage came from—a living being that had to be killed first, no matter how we disguise and cover up those actions and look at those people as second-class citizens, because the people eating those products think they are not involved in the killing. Being knows it is connected to everything. Ego is separate, divided from everything. It lives in a box with a lid on it, and the calamity is it argues that it is not living in a box, the resistance is the giveaway.

Germany dug itself out of the ashes with some help, discipline, sweat, and pain, producing quality products the world started to want. Quality requires alert attention in production, design, and implementation; sadly, this mechanical awakening is not recognized away from work, even today.

Ego makes certain that attention is turned back to me, me, to feed itself with stuff, food, drink, drugs, faster cars, bigger houses. Now, some say greed is good. Germany is not seeing its potential to take its alert attention from work and take it home. Why not use the same quality of alert attention and speak to your wife and children with that positive energy?

Why not?

Immigration

The German military wanted me, to teach me how to kill people; to me, that was too much insanity. Religion told me that Jesus let the masses nail him to the cross so their sins would be forgiven. The capitalist system wanted me to expand forever, till everything was destroyed. The family told me how to live, probably for a long time—a lifetime. That is where the sins of the fathers and mothers repeat themselves: in their children.

About one year and a half after mother's death a letter cam in the mail from the German military to sign up to become a soldier or become a sailor. I decided to become a sailor. Paula, my spiritual mother, had died, and I came home too early; I thought they had forgotten about me.

We educate children to go to war; if we loved our children, we would not educate them to kill other people. Yes, we should not even use the disguises of national security, religion, and other dogmatic excuses, in whose names untold atrocities are committed by simple civil servants.

I had to leave Germany if I didn't want to become a soldier; also, it was an excuse to get away from my father.

The Canadian Consulate in Frankfurt gave me a visa to immigrate to Canada.

One of my friends had an uncle in Vancouver, British Columbia. So I left behind family, friends, love of a kind, my life as I understood it.

My brother drove me to Bremerhaven to go by ocean liner to Canada.

I felt lonely, and tears welled up in my little body as I waved good-bye from the railing, high up on the ship, my brother waving from below on land. It was the first time I felt totally alone; we were soon out in the ocean, surrounded by nothing but water and water for a week.

Yes, it was also exciting to be free, where feeling anything was possible. I did not know then that the present now in a new surrounding is mechanically produced, especially in young people while traveling. Alert attention wells up in one, feeling, seeing, hearing with the whole body, more with being. Like mountain climbers who want that feeling again and again without knowing they can have it anywhere, by going within, making contact with being.

The alert presence is the state without thought!

Ego is never present; it is always in the past or future.

Ego will argue this, will resist this, and will say that it always is in the present.

Moments of presence happen easier in new surroundings, but they are not produced consciously, they only happen. Mountain climbers hanging up a thousand feet on a sheer rock wall have to be present to survive, but they do not know how to create that presence in normal circumstances, the key is alert attention; it can only come from your being, not from your mind. Don't get identified with the words in other righting it is known as, remember yourself always and everywhere. Love is that. Nonresistance acceptance of the present is key, being the formless self is meant by that.

We sailed in the middle of March; we encountered one of those storms, the captain had to go south to avoid icebergs. One time, I looked over the railing, and the waves were almost level with it, the ship moved from side to side. The dining room was mostly empty; by the time we reached Halifax, the ship was covered with ice created by waves slamming against the ship.

In Germany, the Council had told me to go by train to Toronto, but it was so cold I was unable to see the railway station; it was 20 to 30 degrees below zero. I decided to go to Vancouver on the East Coast. That turned out to be a good decision. The never ending trip through the Canadian expanse is too much for words; one feels the magnificence of the earth, its being, the silence in the snow-covered forest, lakes, mountains, villages and towns, endless prairie, space, silence, nothing.

Our own insignificance becomes apparent specially when we ad the universe above to the observation we become very small.

The all powerful Canadian winter makes it more clear how close death is riding along with us. The harsh climate allows few to live there.

After another week by Trans Canada Railway, I reached Vancouver. Traveling across the ocean and a continent for two weeks gave me a perspective of nature, our world, expanses of space and silence.

It is easier to be present while traveling, looking, smelling listening to the new and unexpected. One can say it is a mechanical waking up.

Many people travel the world, but they remain in their mind at home, so they don't really leave home—that is why they complain and judge their new surroundings. Resistance takes us out of the present. That is why Jesus showed us the way of none resistance.

British Columbia

Vancouver is one of the most beautiful cities in the world, and I have asked many a world traveler. The Straits of Juan De Fuqua, Vancouver Island, buffers the BC coast from the cold Northern Pacific; the Coast Range, Garibaldi Park, and the mountain wonderland are all on the doorstep of a city that received its magnificent Stanley Park from an Indian chief, who stipulated never to build houses in it.

The train stopped in Vancouver at eleven o'clock on a Friday morning; by three o'clock, I had work and accommodations.

Stanley Park was the summer playground, Whistler Mountain the heaven in winter. I experienced the space and silence more in Whistler than in the city. I was alone in a new place. It seems that way if you look at it intellectually, but in reality, I was never alone; yes, the mind wants to create depression; in imagination, helpful people and nature are all around, friendships develop quickly, if one wants.

The natural beauty of British Columbia can hardly be described by words like *grand*, *overpowering*, *great*, *magnificent magical*, your being can only experience it if present in the now. So treat words as signposts only;

don't get identified with the word—it is not reality.

Every region in British Columbia has its magnificence my favorites were the mountains and Garibaldi Park, a jewel one can bypass because there is so much of it.

Love is in the details, uninterrupted, formless nonresistance in the present a quality that comes only from formless being in balance with form. There is no yes or no in love only awareness without thought. Love on that level is celibate. There is no celibacy without love.

The trip to Whistler is by itself a trip into wonderland, because of the massive natural impression one can't miss going around every turn.

British Columbia has more logging roads than highways; they are useful for hiking in summer and cross-country skiing in winter. At the time, the excitement of skiing for me was gliding downhill in a controlled way, rhythmically like music, creating swings and presence in the now. Silently gliding through the forest created magic within, connecting with nature. The first conscious shock is conscious breathing; there is no thought, a taste of enlightenment, not understood at the time, because it is mechanically created, like extreme sports. That is for the most part why people go after those activities: they need extreme alert attention to survive. In normal circumstances, you also have this alert attention within you; it is your work to make it conscious in every situation.

While you read this, feel your inner energy body; this makes you more aware of the present. Practice makes present. Those who have to them will be given more. Become aware of your breathing, always and everywhere.

A profession takes three years' apprenticeship; you become a journeyman, then after two more years, you can apply to become a master, and then you are a young master. So after about ten years of intensive work, you become a good master; why do people think going to church once or twice a week is enough to become a master of being, a master of spirit? Jesus didn't work part time.

Why Capitalism Self-Destructs

East Germany was my first home. I experienced that Communist state; the biggest contrast to West Germany for me was almost no invasive advertising, no TV. Yes, we were taught about communism in school. There was some street advertising, depicting the ideal of communism.

One for all, all for one or "Love your neighbor" is the same, isn't it? Communism implemented by corrupt people will fail, the same way corrupt capitalism will fail. After a while in West Germany, the extremely invasive advertising was astounding. All the stuff people bought—more, bigger, faster; expansion forever is the self-destructive ego system.

If people looking at or listening to advertising are not secure within themselves, rooted in their being, the advertised object becomes a self-enhancement object, meaning I have to have it to become more, because I am not complete yet, but if I buy this, I complete myself.

Some people say they complete themselves by having children. Nothing is further from the truth. To be or not to be is still the question. *Not to be* means to go after material belongings and be identified with them—in other words, associating my "I am"

with the object or thought system. I am a ...,
I own a ..., so thought systems and objects
become so enmeshed, "I believe," that is
who I am. The fundamental mistake is the
belief that a thought is not physical it will die
with the body what remains is pure awareness
space eternity.

The second mistake is the illusion of
ownership. The third mistake believing it is the
Achilles heel of humanity.

Ego is built on mistakes—it never has
enough, it always wants more, and it will
destroy itself, similar to a cancer cell.

Capitalism claims free enterprise; for
example, Exxon Mobile, one of the biggest
companies in the world, receives corporate
welfare tax advantages in the billions, while
making billions in profits on its own. Where
are these billions from? Exxon Mobil owns
the patent for the batteries that drove the
EV1 140 miles on one charge; it bought the
patent from General Motors. Do you see the
self-destructive nature of capitalism? GM
would rather destroy itself than build cars
that are good for everyone and for national
security. GM has not changed, the bankers
have not changed.

Ego, with its greed for power, will
destroy its foundation, its natural habitat; it
will build bigger and bigger cities destroy its
food sources poison both the land and the
ocean. Oceans are 80 percent overfished.

Google it: the daily green consumers guide reports studies. Ego can't exist without resistance—that is why it starts wars, for mainly self-enhancement; it will justify those actions mainly from nationalism. It is so easy to excite the masses with fear. When you are in the state of fear, you can't think clearly.

All this information is well known Google it. The daily green consumers guide and other studies. You have to make effort if you want to wake up no one can do it for you. Ego can disproof anything. Your being is needed to find truth. The old system is to slow.

So you will vote for someone who is a warmonger or wastes billions on the military. Then there is nothing left to educate the population. The ruling class isn't interested in a well-educated population, because it is easier to sell stuff to them if they are uneducated. The daily green consumers guide reports studies have found that if fishing is not limited now, there will be no commercial fisheries in 2050. On land, topsoil depletion is a similar problem. The biggest egoic atomic bomb is population explosion.

Why do you have to have children? Children are not the most important thing in a family. You are. They do not complete you.

Ego and capitalism use your insecurity, fear, greed, need for belonging, community, especially that word *belief* made into everything, even belief in capitalism. It is not a sustainable system, because it identifies with its material existence and will never understand being. So it will produce more and more children, so it can destroy itself. That is real evil. That word believe is loved by the ego, it uses it everywhere in Religion if I believe you can tell me any thing as truth. Jesus said I am the way that way is nonresistance, not ego resistance. You can't believe to be present you only can be present now. You can't believe in God you only can be with God in the present formless Now. Jesus said you can do greater things then I, meaning you are his equal on the right hand of God meaning in the present Now with God. God is not separate from you when you are awake conscious present in the formless now you are realized, meaning nonresistant to what is and being one with God.

That is why the study of lies can wake you up out of the dream of thought. In other words the only true job we have is to wake up. You can't resist the present and be in the present. You can not believe that you are awake you have to know that you are awake conscious realized and present.

You are 99.9 percent space within your body and every other body, so go within, and explore the space within, your real self. Be a silent observer, don't judge, and practice nonresistance. You have everything within—go within.

Peace, nonresistance, surrender, love your neighbor, sustainability, one for all, all for one, this also will pass, self-observation, the power of alert attention in the now: none of these exist in capitalism.

Vote with your money! Buy with your being.

You cannot lie, steal, cheat, or pretend not to know—you must be ruthlessly honest with yourself. Belief does not get through the eye of the needle—the belief system is too big, overloaded with stuff and thought.

The rich man is identified with the illusion of ownership. A woman identified with form has insurmountable difficulty with all those bags to pass through the eye of a needle, to get to the kingdom of heaven, which is here and now, not yesterday or tomorrow as written in old books.

Ego is form, formless is being. Ego dose not get into the kingdom of heaven only being is in the kingdom of heaven.

Nonresistance is space, nothing, kindness, external consideration, love for your neighbor, love of silence.

Everything is ONE. Nothing is separate.

Jesus did not say, "Nail me to the cross, so your sins will be forgiven"; he showed the way of nonresistance, in the kingdom of heaven, the present, now.

In capitalism, expansion can't be sustained; its self-destruction is what we call waking sleep. Ego never has enough, always wants more, and will destroy itself. Desire for sustainability is the answer, the middle way. Clean energy comes from Being, dirty energy is ego.

If we don't wake out of the dream of thought, capitalism will continue destroying the planet.

Jesus did not die on the cross to forgive your destructive behavior; he showed the way not be destructive. Nonresistance is the strongest force in the universe—it is your real self.

Capitalism is ego; it does not, will never be, can only do, is only the mind—the best computer on the planet—but only that. It cannot be creative; it only pretends to be creative. Creativity comes from being. Striving for profit the Goldman Sachs way is planning to destroy, living on weaknesses, not helping others to grow in the middle way. Taking advantage of weakness is ego, insanity, criminal, smart, but not intelligent.

You can profit from what is good for all and make a very good living. Goldman Sachs is smart in hatching out how to profit from the weak, not intelligent; it is self-destructive. Drilling for oil offshore is smart; the same amount of dollars spent on renewable energy is intelligent, because it is renewable, while oil is dirty, pollutes, and is finite. Why pour dollars into a black hole? Not intelligent. That is how capitalismself-destructs:itthrivesonresistance. Without resistance, it cannot exist; it creates war and fear so it can exist in a destructive way. It has no conscience, it is sleep—one can call it waking sleep. Capitalism can't see its self-destructive ways. Gurdjieff said; the lower can't see the higher.

In the Name of National Security

What is national security? A nation that lives in peace with its neighbors, knowing that "all for one, one for all" is the same as loving your neighbor.

A family lives under one roof, lives with its differences has its rules to exist within and without. If a neighbor injures, damages, or kills one of your families you don't go out and kill the neighborhood. The law of the land, or nations, takes over.

Take the 9/11 tragedy as an example.

The right course of action was to consult with the United Nations and decide what the course of action must be, because people removed from the situation have a clearer picture of the whole. Revenge, retaliation, violence creates more of the same. It is pouring from the empty into the void, unintelligent. Approximately two thousand people were killed in New York; thirty thousand children die of hunger every day, thousands of smokers die each day on the planet, but because we don't see it in a big event like New York, we don't care, unintelligent. Genocide in Africa: again, thousands die, no reaction to stop it in America.

For a short time, the world was behind America after 9/11; the world, the United

Nations were waiting for America to sit down and work out a plan to deal with the problem. But America was not ready, not awake, to lead the world in an enlightened way; the opposite happened, the United States took the primitive way of revenge as a disguise for attacking a neighbor, pulling the world back to the Middle Ages, not intelligent.

American national security is bad by any standard, because violence creates more violence. What you fight you strengthen; you become what you fight, in time. America is that now. The new government tries to reverse the old destructive course, with much opposition from the old.

War must be the last resort, if all other possible solutions are exhausted.

National security can only come from within; peace within the individual translates to peace within the relationship, to peace within the family, the nation, the world.

National security will not come from governments it must come from the individual.

Only when we die to the past will we be peace in the Now.

This truth of dying to the past must be acted on by the individual in order to be in the Now. If the past has any hold, identification, addiction over me, I cannot be in the present.

One question can be, how nonresistant I am now, because resistance is always ego. Ego is form. Being is formless.

The way of love can also be called the way of nonresistance.

Death and love are one. You can't be present if you have not died to your past. Be in this world, but not of it.

When pain becomes conscious, ego dies. Ego needs resistance to exist, ego creates pain. So it starts a war, in a relationship, family, workplace, or nation. Ego hides behind national security to justify raping, killing, cheating, stealing, destroying anything in the end, even itself that it can't comprehend because it lives in a box with a lid on it, called a self-imposed prison. *Identification, sleep, vanity, self-aggrandizement, delusion, dogmatic thinking*, and *dream of thought* are some words describing the state of living in a box it is a form of insanity.

Kindness, compassion, conscious, nurturing, joyful, equal, ethical, fair, forgiving, sharing, spiritual, to name a few attributes, are not in the ego's lifestyle. Since about 99 percent of government employees, including the president and the private sector are ruled by their ego, the national security policy is also ruled by ego. Any system that is not inclusive giving everybody the same level playing field will destroy it self. Look at Egypt. Our government leaders are not spiritual.

Is the Truth Hidden or Available?

Who is asking?

Everyone is not on the same level of awareness.

In the absence of that which you are not, that which you are is not.

If you are asking with patience, you will get the answer when you are ready to receive. It can take years to get an answer. Do not expect the answer to only come in one way.

The truth of men or women, number one to five or beyond, must be different by nature of limited understanding and level of being.

The observation of your body and thoughts tells you that you are not the observed but the observer. That is why it is useful to know what type you are; don't confuse type with your real self, the observer, the intelligence which is actually operating, healing, growing, declining, controlling your body is not your brain or thought, it is that intelligence which operates your body including your brain. It is that intelligence operating the universe. Scientists will never find it because it is not material. They can make that collider in Switzerland twice as big cant find the nothing with ego. They are looking for the intelligence that builds that machine and themselves.

Ego is smart, not intelligent. Intelligence includes all and everything, not only what is inside the box; the ego claims it thinks outside the box, but that doesn't make it so.

Instinctive types are often employed in the food industry; they react instinctively to situations; for instance the understanding of food may be more important than other activities. These types have an instinctive understanding of the body's working. They are underdeveloped in emotional perception and intellectual pursuits, good at sports activities. This is a broad brushstroke here; more detail can be found in Gurdjieff Euspensky's books. A stack of playing cards is used to illustrate more in detail. You are a jack, queen, or king. Type has no advantage in waking up.

Instinctive Type:	Clubs, instinctive decision making
Moving Type:	Spades, decisions related to movement
Intellectual Type:	Diamonds, slow, intellectual decision making
Emotional Type:	Hearts, fast, emotional decision making

You are born with a center of gravity, where most of your mechanical decisions are made from; one can also call it stimulus response.

Chief feature is power, vanity, and nonexistence.

It is easy to get identified with a big system like the fourth way or any religion or party. Don't forget that the truth is in simplicity.

What you seek tomorrow will never come, because it is always now.

Don't seek enlightenment; become present now.

The truth is in the present, not yesterday or tomorrow.

Jesus did not say to love your neighbor tomorrow.

Let it be, in the now. Allow you're self to be in the now. Nonresistance is the way to truth, which is only in the now. You know the truth if you are in the formless now. The truth is not hidden from anybody, but if you are not in the present now, the truth may as well be behind a big mountain or on the moon. In the not so distant past people where burned on the stakes for saying or writing what is in this book.

When women copy the lifestyle of men, that doesn't elevate women or lift them to the level of men's power, it makes women as insane as men.

When you choose a career and go from apprentice to journeyman, all the way to master, you have mastered something very well. Three years apprentice, three years journeyman, and then you have the possibility of becoming a master. A beginning master. Masters can be in this world but not of it, meaning they penetrated the formless present moment and are alertly present, in the formless now, without attachments, identifications, or judgments. Nothing of quality can be produced if you are not in the now. The famous Harvard-educated bankers are on the level of apprentice; ripping off the masses in a sly formulated system is not intelligent, is not on the level of a master; they don't know the responsibility for all, so they miss the present and work in the past and future.

The apprentice, charging ahead, thinking, not being, getting into difficulty, says, "I can't get rid of the ghosts I called." (Goethe) Why? The answer is, to be in ego, or not to be in ego. Not of this world is formless being. Ego is form-based thinking, and doing is stimulus response.

There is form-based attention and formless attention; the apprentice is mostly in form-based attention, masters can be mostly in formless attention if they are realized, which means in unity and nonresistance.

Being removes mountains, ego builds imaginary mountains.

The truth changes with your perception or level of being.

The perceiver, the silent observer, that which is not affected by drama or negativity, is silence. The intelligence, the knowing, the nonjudgmental, formless silent observer within you, is available to you now.

You become one with the problem, which means you are present without blaming judging and acceptance of the now.

When spirituality becomes a teaching, in a small way it will be being, the bigger the teaching becomes, the more ego enters the teaching, misunderstandings and complexities enter, simplicity of the now is covered up, mostly by ego. When you are in the formless presence of now, you are the truth, and you know it. To being nothing is hidden. To ego, everything is hidden in denying the present and pretending to understand, arguing when there is nothing to argue about.

Communism and Other Confusions

When you have lived in a Communist country and then move to a Western capitalist country, your perspective may differ according to your experience, driven by your own energy level. Resistance creates more resistance, in other words, when you resist what is, your life becomes more difficult. That is true for a person, family, or country. We are not sent to planet earth to change it, possibly to manage the earth, help, but not destroy. The ideal of communism is superior to the destructive perpetual slash and burn for profit capitalism.

"One for all, all for one" is "love your neighbor."

The individual striving for the imaginary top is that: imaginary. The American dream is that: a dream, a thought. A dream is not in the present; belief in a dream is not the same as knowing that you have the present now.

Both systems reveal their weakness of wanting to go to the top, or wanting to love the neighbor. Both systems are failures because of not understanding, being in the present.

Both systems operate in the past or future, even forgetting the value of the individual. The computer is king, it operates by numbers. Being is not numbers it is the formless observer observing the numbers and not being influenced by the numbers. Ego is form, being is formless.

Capitalism—with its glitz, smoke and mirrors, snake oil sales tactics—speaks to the lower energy centers of the population: greed, fear, instant gratification.

Capitalism in the United States loves to keep the population undereducated. It is easier to sell uneducated people stuff they don't need, or operate an outdated energy system, even if that system causes destruction on a big scale.

For the educated classes, capitalism makes expensive stuff: overpriced cars and houses, food to satisfy the upper class's expensive, needy, self-destructive ego systems, bloated military, bigger and bigger corporations and that creates oversized lobbying groups all in a self-destructive mode.

The confusion is not that we don't know; we only pretend that we don't know.

All solutions are given to us; humanity has all the answers, but we prefer not to use them. Humanity prefers to live in the past and future, knowing that they do not exist.

The dream of thought, so powerful for thousands of years, is not going away by itself, like the second coming of Jesus, which so many want to believe is not going to happen, because there is only now. Communism, capitalism, organized religion—many want to believe in one or the other; whatever system you believe in, especially if that belief lasts longer than about seven years, becomes your prison you walked into willingly, because the law of mass takes over and your relatively small amount of thought energy is no match for the big-time energy of any religion, capitalism, communism, Democrat, Republican, or any big thought system; you become that system. You lose your self.

My advice: leave your favorite club for a while and look at it from the outside.

Then you may see that those clubs are actually keeping you from being in the present now, by encouraging you to believe in salvation tomorrow and believing in the past. The present is filled with fear about the devil and hell, commandments, laws, judgment, blaming, even a vengeful God.

Jesus taught the opposite of that Being the formless Now simplicity. Love your neighbor one for all all for one is the same. Look at the lily in the field or a tree; a dog can teach you what being is.

The systems have not turned on themselves—the people managing them misunderstood Jesus. You can go all the way back to the Apostles Peter and Paul; it seems they did not understand Jesus' teaching, and that is why they pushed Mary out of her rightful role as leader.

The Christian system has not turned on itself; the leader's right from the beginning after Jesus' death misunderstood his teaching (except possibly Mary).

The corrupted change of direction comes from the leaders of all those systems.

They were unable to see their own ego for what it was after the spiritual energy of Jesus was gone. They reverted back to their old jealous fighting, quibbling, blaming, "ego self."

Buddhism is possibly one of the least contaminated systems.

Presently, no religions are needed; they demonstrated failure on a grand scale.

The individual is called upon to go within and reassemble the total being. It must be understood by each individual and can't be implemented by any religion or system; it is totally individual, like breathing, but as soon as the understanding is present, that all is connected.

One has to be ruthlessly honest with oneself in observing one's thoughts, emotions, and actions in the present, not yesterday or tomorrow.

Humanity is going beyond belief, now is the present, you can't believe that you are present you can only be in the present.

Everything has been written about all different types of understanding, angles, vibrations, viewpoints. Everything has been said before, in one way or another nothing is new in formation, we have been told all that is written here for thousands of years, humanity prefers not to remember and listen.

Resistance fighters are not needed—what you resist persists.

Look at Cuba: on the surface it looks like communism prevailed. Yes, the system changed from one group of people to another; the old "I have the power, you do what I tell you" is law. What changed was a power shift, different people with different words and clothing, no true freedom.

No spiritual solution was found or implemented.

Alcoholics Anonymous knows there is no cure without spirituality.

In an individual or nation, the same laws apply. There is no Nation with a spiritual lieder religious yes. In the name of national security, more crimes are committed by civil servants and elected officials than any individual ever can commit; 99 percent of the world population is totally in ego. Should you be interested in the 1 percent, look to Alcoholics Anonymous, the people who made contact with their spiritual self and are on the way out of the dream of thought, reassembling themselves so to speak; healing; becoming whole; waking up, out of the dream of thought.

As long as America is killing people, it will regress, and that goes for all nations. Any organization condoning, justifying, or encouraging the killing of humans by law is forcing itself to live in and from the lower chakras and cannot live up to its potential. It can talk about peace but not implement it. You can't do peace you only can "be" peace.

Israel, you can talk peace but not implement peace.

You have to *be* peace, and you only can be peace within your formless self. Forgive. Die to the past. Jesus showed the way of nonresistance.

Only then can you be in the present now—that is where peace is. That is the meaning of Being.

Peace can't be created by organizations—communism, capitalism, religions—it only can be in the individual formless being, and so be and grow into a relationship, family, town, nation.

Realization means no separation, no resistance.

Self-Destruction in Disguise

A lot of people are in negative states almost all the time because of
drugs, ego, power, addictions, nationalism, believing, identification, resistance, constantly thinking, depression are all more or less negative self-destructive expressions.

Dissatisfaction, complaining, and judgment all seem based on rightful analysis of a situation, and my dissatisfaction and negativity with now seems justified.

The same with complaining: I complain about a wrong somebody does to me or did to me a long time ago.

I judge a situation in a relationship where the other is clearly wrong from my point of view. That is all it is: a point of view. Study the art of non expression of negative emotions it will heal your mind body and soul.

Justified blaming is the ego's way of saying "I am better than you, and we are not connected; you are separate from me." This internalized blaming game can go on all the time; if not recognized for what it is it will cause depression and illness, an unrecognized form of self-destruction.

This is true in a one-on-one relationship as well as in the family, town, business, state, and country. We go to war, because someone makes a big story out of a relatively small incident because he wants to justify his superiority over others; for that, the ego kills in the name of peace, national security, Jesus, God, Mohamed, Buddha, any god that comes to mind. The mind will distort any situation, using any means at its disposal to justify its position. You can call it ego insanity.

This is true for all negative emotions. The emotion jealousy in its extreme states is extremely destructive, people have killed for it. Nations have started wars, individuals have become insane. That is why nations are also insane when they start a war, but it is disguised as national security or such a self-destruction in disguise.

Greed, one of the most common forms of self-destruction because it is so elusive, comes in so many disguises. Greed for food—hunger, greed for instant gratification—self-worth, greed for sex—population explosion (possibly one of humanity's greatest problems), greed for money—self-aggrandizement, security, force, greed for fame—destruction of spirit, all is destruction of spirit, we can go on and on. The ego can't see any of it, will argue it away and feel justified in winning the argument, because being will not resist, is formless, understands ego, will let ego play itself out of energy. Being allows ego.

Ego does not understand itself, it is the most complex and smart computer, ego is not creative it moves numbers around, very complex. But that is not creative. Creativity only comes from your formless self when you are still, silent, empty of thought. You can't put anything in a full glass.

Greed for money on Wall Street is accepted as a good thing by many; being is totally disregarded, ego has taken over.

This self-destructive behavior is easier seen in others than in oneself, because alert stillness in the present now is required to observe one's own thoughts and behavior. One has to refine one's energy to be present.

As long as one is lying to oneself, development is digressing.

Suffering consciously—that is, without blaming and judging—is a good start to lessen the force of ego.

Become aware of your breathing. Meditate in your own way. Acceptance of what is embraces the present; it is healing and uniting, as long as no harm is done to anyone. When suffering becomes conscious, the ego loses force.

Nonresistance in your daily activities will relieve stress and illness. It is the way back from self-destruction. In this present alert state, within this inner silence is the peace you have been looking for everywhere; you will not find it in your thought systems, religions, or younger lover.

What Does Sex Have to Do with It?

Sexual energy is the motor of life. Some say everything is sex. Yin and yang born into form, we can say that there are different understandings of sex.

The confusion is that not only are we of different types, we are also of different vibrations', meaning development. Not everybody is a Stradivari, but in its essence, formless self everyone is equal. The only reason we cam to this planet is to wake up out of the dream of thought, that started a very long time ago. Not that much can happen in one lifetime. Our general problem is that we become identified with systems sentences words and of course sex and most about everything else. It has been said that Nature will always win. That doesn't mean you can't observe and by observing every time lessen the identification.

To speak of sex of man or woman number 1, 2, 3, 4, 5, and so on in general terms is confusing, because who is speaking, of what kind of sex. It is like pouring from the empty into the void.

For man number one, moving instinctive man, it is animal sex.

Have to have children to feel accomplishment, propagate to live the illusion of continuation. There is only degeneration in the material world everything comes and goes.

Intellectually centered man has sex in his head more than others. Loves to read and looses him self in thought imagination, wants to think about everything, has mostly intellectual connection to people. Thoughts are his world, believes that that is real.

The solar plexus is the center of gravity for man number three—emotion. Emotional people are naturally overweight to buffer those fast volatile mostly negative emotions. The queen of harts in Allis in Wonderland is an example.

The glimpses of awakening for man number four change everything. He observes energy pulse through the body when more awake, present, alert begins to feel inner space. Awakening may be only seconds in the beginning but it sets a trend once started you cant go back. Awareness and thought start to separate creating space to be aware without thinking. Man number four can be any type. Any type can wake up once realized that waking sleep is the insanity of humanity. He becomes the observer of his thoughts, knows he is not his thoughts. But man number four and fife can loose all that. All the recommended reading in the back of the book has more information from different angles.

George Gurdjieff brought the" Fourth Way" to the west to help wake western man from his waking sleep it is also called the" Work " because nothing happens by itself. Attention on breathing needs energy if I waist my energy on negativity getting up in the morning because I was dissalisfied with sex I had or any lhing that "made me " negative, there may be no energy left to be present, for the rest of the whole day. That is why you say you had a bad day. In reality there are no bad days or good days. The present is the present, with sex or without it. To remember the next day that I want to wake up I have to set myself alarm clocks so to speak.

When identified with form, life, there is nobody home.

Sex becomes a tool lo awaken; with alert presence, he or she uses the energy of wanting the imaginary lover to perform in the past or future, in this never-ending movie of ego love, to be in the now, accepts its outcome without complaining or aggrandizement.

The connection to everything is awakened; in other words, we jump out of the box, observation without thought becomes clearer,

While engaged in any activity, have a part of your attention on your breathing; this opens a door to feeling the energy of the inner body as often as possible and brings you into the present; awareness of place and space is enlarging, because of alert presence, only then are we beginning to be human beings rediscovering the formless self. In other words reassemble your self, you are only developed ego, your being has been forgotten.

Without presence, we are stimulus response machines. Sex addiction does not make us more awake; like any addiction, we are more and more identified with it, living inside the box.

When you are coming from being your formless self or soul, you can't be identified with your lower chakras.

You are not minding what is happening, you are in this world but not of it.

It doesn't mean you don't care. The opposite is true.

When there is resistance, deviousness, manipulation, and competition at play, sex is only another ego game. Love does none of that.

Lower sex energies are dividing, while higher sex energies are uniting.

Sex energy used in the lower chakras are more like ego games and are not inclusive but mostly self enhancement.

Without beauty, there is no love. Beauty is not a beautiful flower, tree, building, or woman. There is beauty only when you see beauty with your being. Beauty is everywhere. Being sees beauty in a forest untouched by man. There is no beginning and no end; the living, loving, and dying merge into one. Love is never yesterday or tomorrow; it can only be in the present now. It is not love, wanting to be with a special someone with conditions attached. You can't love if you don't die to the past, within yourself.

Are We Capable of Seeing the Big Picture

Gourdjieffs Fourth Way system is difficult he is giving you work to find answers for your self.

In the book *The Secret,* the answer is given but still difficult to understand. In the book *The Power of Now*, the same is pointed to in more detail. In the book *Living and Dying*, the truth is set free. In the book *A New Earth*, the truth is laid out like hiking trails in the mountains, with directional signs in important places and detailed explanations and long awareness of truths. Gurdjief cam to the west in the beginning of the century people where not ready for simplicity. Jesus taught simplicity look what they did to him.

Wecan'tbeinthenowandcomplaining. What is the now to an individual? What is awareness ?

Alert attention is the key. If we waste our energy on complaining, judging, resisting what is, lying, manipulating, drugs to cover up what is, it will be as difficult to be present as a camel passing through the eye of a needle.

How can we not waste energy so we can be aware and see the big picture? The lower charkas—red, orange, yellow-gold—waste energy if not connected to higher chakras. Bad food or too much food makes it difficult to be present. Using meditation attention on breathing, walking in the forest, alert attention without naming everything—these will bring you into the present, give you a taste of the present; then awareness changes from identification to presence because your observation is not compartmentalized. You start to look outside the box. This is why the occult is also called "The Work" a inner effort is required to get out of the apprentice period, acceptance is key foundation to refine your energy to the middle way so you don't get trapped in complaining and judging any more.

There is only a limited amount of energy in a day.

Any addiction takes us away from the now, because craving, wanting in excess, is identification with the past or future, is not satisfied with the middle way. Allowing and bearing the pain of not having sets you free.

Liebe ist die Kleinichkeit: Love is in the detail. Presence is in the detail. In other words, the detail is connected to the whole.

What is the big picture? It must include the formless. Being is the creator of form, the creative, the inner self, the intelligence. Don't only look at things—look at the space in between, raise your head and look at the universe as often as possible, create space for your own Being. When you have a bad day, the children don't want to listen to you, the wife makes unreasonable demands at work the boss screams at you, can you stay calm your reaction tells you the level of being you are.

That picture also tells us where we stand in relationship to consciousness. Are we an apprentice, a journeyman, or a master? How do we know? When the going gets tough—the stock market goes down, the wife makes unreasonable demands, the children resist your words, everything goes wrong at work—can you stay calm, instead of fighting the situation? Can you merge with it intelligently, creatively solve it? You can see your progress or regression in difficult situations, see where you stand. It is always easier to see in others. The key is alert attention. So we can see the big picture only if we are awake, or we are coming from being, our inner self. The ego will disguise itself as being, but it can never be, because it is form. Ego can't see its true nature; only being can observe and be in the totality, eternity. Formless Now is also called heaven.

The pursuit of constant activity: sports, TV, games, sex, food, reading, rote learning. Attention deficit disorder is mostly the result of parents having no love for the child, because what you don't have you can't give. Read study the modern healing Prophet Edgar Cayce and all the books recommended. The question is the answer, you can't do love only be love.

The books recommended speak about love and healing, where illnesses com from in more detail. Everything is given I cant make you have it, nobody can make you conscious you cant buy self-realization the first is given by grace then you are making contact with your own inner self: "acceptance, joy and passion" without dose we are only stimulus response machines-ego. Science will never find being, it is the intelligence it is looking for, you can't find that what you are, if you are asleep to your real self it mid as well be on the moon. Put attention on your breathing that gives you a little separation between awareness and thought, that separation is your first realization that you are not your thought.

Thinking, without love in your heart, (ego) will keep you from seeing the truth. In other words, you are in ego, inside the box with a lid on it, in this physical world of thought, dogma identification. Some call this love these negative states are creating illnesses in different degrees for people.

This lying to your self in different gradations of negativity is causing most illnesses, the person is mostly out of balance with its inner vibrations, in other words the orchestra plays wrong notes all the time, this causes mental and physical illnesses. Ego will always create more pain if it is the primary force in your life. In reality being is the primary force.

Saying I love you all the time means nothing, children know that.

Look at space, look around objects, and observe the night sky. While you eat, be aware of space around you. This will create inner space, intelligence.

Meditate, pay attention to your breathing, feel your heart pump blood through your body; wherever you are is a start to go within where formless, limitless intelligence in the present formless now is connected to all and everything. Jesus said: the kingdom of heaven is within you, presence in the Present Now.

When you begin to feel your inner being, your outer is accepted as it is without complaining, judging; it is accepted as it is understood as it is.

Nonresistance to the present now makes you aware of the power of love. All this is written about in the books recommended in a more understandable form than agent writings and others in the tradition of Esotericism, despised by ego. You can't do the now only be in the now. Esotericism existed long before there where books and pyramids.

John 14: 6 Jesus answered: I am the way truth and the life (which are spiritually speaking the same--- consciousness--- life,

Nature God are all the same) no one comes to the Father (consciousness being god) but by me (consciousness present now) which is space consciousness nonresistance, acceptance, joy, passion. They are only words, go beyond the word! Be the word. Awareness without thinking is what Einstein eluted to when he said; Scientists have no problem thinking, there problem is how not to think. When awareness separates from thought it is called awakening by Tolle.

As described earlier it takes a minimum of ten years to become a master why people think reading a book is all it takes. Going to church can be regressive is the opposite what it takes to wake up. Belief it looks like is putting people to sleep making sheep out of people, followers don't wake up they do what is written or what they are told. Belief nothing verify everything for your self. Nobody can wake anybody up, you can ask, but are you ready to accept the foundation of waking up which is acceptance of the present now as it is. The ego will find a way to make this into an argument, being will let it, because ego is showing its level of consciousness. We are showing our level of consciousness by our actions.

Can We Stop Believing?

Believing in God is childish. Religions need believers, believers become followers, and followers believe what they are told.

Belief is destroying the earth and humanity. Western religion believes Jesus died on the cross for you, so your sins are forgiven! Jesus was nailed to the cross by egomaniacs, living today as much as they lived then, propagating the same falsehood, because they are coming from ego and have nothing to do with spirituality.

Jesus did not say, "I die on the cross for you." He said: John 14 6

"I am the way," and that way is the way of nonresistance. Jesus did not resist!

Resistance is the way of the ego!

Believers have been exploited for a long time with this falsehood. We are afraid to look, not wanting to see truth. It is much easier to follow a system and hide behind it, faking it as truth, arguing for falsehood.

"The ego is always right, never makes a mistake, and will destroy itself."

Similar to the cancer cell, smart but not intelligent, the bankers are smart but not intelligent. They only understand a system; they have no comprehension of the whole. There on the level of a beginning apprentice.

Ego believes, being knows. Ego is fear, but being knows the truth within can't be put into words because it is formless.

Do you believe in war? If you loved your children, you would have no war!

Because the way you educate your children is a preparation for war.

You only pretend to love your children. You are only pretending to love.

If you truly loved your children, you would not send them into war.

Creativity comes from being. Being is always in the present. "I believe in God" is expressed as a thought by 95 percent of humanity. I know God can only be expressed by being, the formless. Not to long ago you where burnet at the stakes if you said that.

Belief is a thought projected from the past into the future, trying to make it real, pretending that the past is not dead. The pictures in your head are only a movie, like a dream, a movie playing in your head. Nothing wrong with thinking if it is secondary, awareness without thought must be primary to be love, which is always in the present.

Some commuters spend $500 to $1,000 per month on gasoline—that is approximately $5,000 to $10,000 in one year, $50,000 to $100,000 in only ten years, and $100,000 to $200,000 in twenty years!

So a hybrid car is the answer, I have been told (in two years or less). A solar installation on your roof looks inexpensive; even if you have to buy new batteries after twenty years, you can afford it.

The solar installation with the electric car, $50,000 paid off in ten years. After twenty years, you have saved $50,000 to $100,000.

The argument that you need new batteries is childish!

Your cars need gasoline, oil, maintenance.

Your solar installation and your electric car need very little maintenance. All components are now recycled.

Halleluiah, you have become a responsible citizen of the universe.

For long-distance travel, you can buy a hybrid; in two years, there will be many choices. You can rent a car for long-distance travel. Better yet, buy a diesel hybrid if you can.

Solar installations and electric cars are available with a small down payment.

You have completed a positive long thought and put a big question mark on dirty old energy.

Don't dwell on that thought; go back to awareness, joy and passion.

Dirty energy is ego, while clean energy comes from being—it is good for all, including the earth. Tesla, the man, is clean energy; he had seven hundred patents in his name. Not Edison or Marconi. They stole his inventions.

Quote from Edison: "Everybody steals in commerce and industry. I've stolen a lot myself. But I know how to steal!" Sounds like dirty energy to me!

Ego uses belief to make you feel competent, that you are in the know, that you belong, but if you lift the lid off the box and start to observe those thoughts, you begin to see what they are: smoke and mirrors lying to one self. The observer is the observed—there is no separation. Ego must be separate to exist. Ego loves to say, "I know."

To use dirty explosive energy generation requires believing that it will do no harm to humanity and the universe. Clean implosion energy, (Tesla) possibly knew the truth about the universe.

The universe is electric implosion energy (Tesla). Go within yourself and feel the power within; belief (ego) will argue this truth away. Belief cannot sustain itself in the present; it lives in the past and future, in the dream of thought. Be present and not waste your energy on some useless instant gratification. Ego can't look outside the box. Ego will never understand being; it can only falsify and lie about being.

Being will not resist. Being can't be destroyed—it is eternity. At fifty years of age, I had a big problem: my body was breaking down fast. My body became stiff; my legs, arms, and back became alarmingly stiff; getting dressed became painful. One night my wife had to rush me to the hospital because of an allergic reaction to penicillin. There was swelling of the body all over, including the windpipe. Breathing became critical.

After I was home again, I decided to make some big changes in my lifestyle.

For an experiment, I stopped eating beef and pork. After a month, I felt improvement, so I stopped eating fish and chicken. After three months, the improvement was pronounced. I was able to move my body again, and I felt fitter, able to think and work better. I added a walking program to exercises, and the healing in mind, body, and spirit was nothing but remarkable.

We make one mistake: we take too many vitamin pills. Hot castor oil compresses on painful body parts help a great deal. But after that correction, health returned pronouncedly.

Again, belief is childish; listen to your body—each cell is intelligently connected to the electric magnetic waves, to all the space in the whole universe, where true intelligent resides.

Your body is 99.9 percent space—this is important.

Edgar Cayce the great American Prophet of the new age and healer can be of help on the subject of healing in any area of the body and mind. There are Doctors realizing his healings where all recorded and using that material in there work to day. When are we using what is given?

Is Your Formless Self Stronger than Your Ego?

The question is, to be or not to be. Ego is form, being is formless. Ego is smart, being is intelligent.

Humanity is 99 percent in ego most of the time, it does not know being, identification with ego is almost total. Form-based thinking is that.

These are some of the ways of being, non resistance, kindness, selflessness, intelligence, invisibility, external consideration love for your neighbor.

Jesus showed the way of not resisting; not the resurrection story   invented by old white men. Not by the one who understood Jesus: Mary.

Ego is all smart show, smoke and mirrors, snake oil sales—any method is good if it brings more power and money. Ego never has enough, always wants more, and will destroy itself. The bankers are all ego, which works like a cancer cell—it will destroy itself. Not intelligent!

Most creators of the last banking collapse, came from Harvard—it's no accident. Unfortunately, most of Obama's administration is from Harvard or Goldman Sachs , they are mostly ego based, gave billions of taxpayers dollars to the banks the creators of criminal snake oil sales to the masses made the laws in there own favor, like the Cigarette CEOS pretended not to know. What are they getting million bonuses paid for?

From Atlantis to today, all other smaller civilizations have destroyed themselves; doesn't that tell you that ego is a destruction machine? By the way, all were controlled by men.

But ego can't look outside the box, , in other words it is a nonissue because it can't see itself. Ego is dirty energy—Edison, J. P. Morgan, Rockefeller, big oil, coal. Nobody makes a serious study of the effect oil extraction has on the earth's crust; pumping water back is not the same apparently.

Atomic energy works on the explosion principle, egoic expansion it has no respect for life, will destroy everything for a profit, creates war to sustain itself, and needs conflict to exist. That is why so many couples get divorced: only ego is present, no being; all me, me, me; resistance to all or most lifestyles of the other; little cooperation leads to division.

The idea of nationalism creates war, we have to get rid of borders to the peace, within ourselves don't allow borders to nationalism to be exposed for what they are: narrow-minded, insane.

Most decisions are form based, in the past or future. The ego can't live in the present, so the present is called unimportant or argued away: we will solve that problem later, or we will talk that over next week; there is no next week, only now. When you talk about the problem again, it will be now again, the changes can be enormous in one week.

Change is the only constant in the universe.

The ego and all form-based systems, including thought, will die.

Formless intelligence, the present now, is all you have, within.

The more ordinary you are, the more invisible, your one-on-one work has possibility. The ego gets hold of you, stuffs you into a meat grinder, and spits you out, happens to the rich, famous, poor, and everybody not being present. Not knowing that it is happening.

Being is clean energy, solar, wind, sun, renewable energy. It respects life, does not destroy haphazardly.

The world's renewable energy is at 1 percent, about the same percentage as people working with being.

Recorded and unrecorded time shows us destruction of all those civilizations; none survived, some cities sunk into the ocean. Buildings constructed five thousand to ten thousand years ago or more, and totally misinterpreted by our ego civilization.

The first pyramid was a big generator producing energy by implosion (Tesla), dirty energy, destroys itself. Clean implosion energy creates, similar to being, it is creative, speaks the truth, dirty energy is destructive, lies, hides behind thick doors, national security or other excuses. Dirty energy creates war. The universe is run by clean energy, electric implosion energy. Can you see the universe run by oil?

Belief is dirty oil, being is clean implosion electric energy.

After the universe or the solar system has imploded, the silent space remains.

Belief Sleep

Are we forcing children, educating children, into a form of "belief sleep"?

You can't love your children and teach them to go to war and kill.

Why do we not love our children? So are the sins of fathers and mothers revisited upon the children for a thousand years.

Do we know what love is? Do we love ourselves? No strings attached, no conditions, in the present, not tomorrow or yesterday—now.

Love is in the present detail.

Are we serious with children, without blaming, no negativity?

Can we be with them seriously, not dream or working on something else, be there, let them be? Not telling children what to do all the time. Observe them; protect them without overbearing behavior.

Can we be serious, honest, not in the yes or no position, rather the golden middle of understanding and knowing? Not the usual stimulus response machine.

Don't children deserve alert attention now? They give it to you, till we destroy it, stuff it into a bottle, and seal it with steel. Ego can't stand being.

So you teach them the way of the ego, and you complain that they don't turn out the way you want them to.

Ego is always right, never has enough, always wants more, and will destroy itself. Sound familiar?

Here is this old truth, said a thousand times: to be or not to be.

How to be in the golden middle takes work—it doesn't just happen.

Not to be happens, is a stimulus response, is ego mechanical physical.

Life is real only when I am awake, out of the dream of thought.

That is the nonresistant inner state, called realization.

Everything is one; there is no resistance.

Be and watch your child in that state as long as you can—make a practice of it.

Your being knows truth; your ego will talk you out of it.

Why not teach your children being? They are going to get plenty from everybody else's ego.

Being is formless love. Love is formless being.

Nonresistance, the Strongest Power in the Universe

Jesus showed us the way of nonresistance, so did the Buddha.

Why is humanity so violent with itself? War is insanity. Domination is insanity.

Politicians, ordering it in the name of this or that, are insane, behind a veil, a burka. Lying, cheating, stealing, and meat consumption go with killing; these actions are raping in one form or another. Politicians hide behind fancy words like *national security*, *defense, life style*. The atrocities committed by the collective are far greater than those committed by individuals.

Why does humanity self-destruct? Is it because it is afraid to die, so it kills others? The word *humanity* is not applicable yet! We are still copying the ways of animals, 99 percent of which want to be humans.

The sins of the mothers and fathers repeat themselves for a million years, to this day. Those sins are getting trapped in materiality (ego), forgetting being, destroying the female principal elevating male dominance, educating the young for war competition, deceiving killing.

People are trapped in the dream of thought.

We still believe we can fight our way out of problems—the war on drugs, the war on illness, the war on terror, the war on this and the other.

The result of all this warring is getting worse, so we continue, because we are really bad at observing ourselves.

What you fight you strengthen; what you resist persists! These are natural laws. If you fight something, you create more pain for all involved, and you become what you fight.

Why don't we stop fighting? Nonresistance is not weakness, as Jesus showed us. What can a sane person achieve with $ 100 billion going into Iraq without weapons?

Human beings can't kill one another! Only animals do. If we want to become human beings, then we have to stop the activity, ways of animals.

The habit of slaughtering animals must be reduced greatly if humanity wants to survive a little longer and reduce the pain it produces for itself.

We also have to stop eating animals the way people do, it may produce violence and illness. They are beings like we are. Everything is conscious, even a stone. God is everywhere; you can't avoid her, him, it.

You shall not kill is not a commandment, it is a guideline like all scriptures, holy or not, to help us on our way to the now. God never gave commandments, God gives guidelines, street signs for us to follow if we want to know God. God is not a dictator!

Live your life from the present, be hear now.

Truth is your formless self out of which you came and will return. Life is in the present now. Your body will die in the now, not in the past or future. There is no love without death.

Every death is showing we die in the now, we give up everything, including the body and breathing.

Forgiveness, humility, kindness, external consideration, inclusion, alert presence, and conscious breathing are creating actions of nonresistance and may lead to insights that are not thinking, as it is understood in the normal context. Silence, nothing, space can't be quantified—that is why it is the beauty, intelligence, and truth everyone has within, and we can only live it if dying to the past and future is lived. If we die to the past, what remains is being. The question is do we want to be or not to be. We can be present at our death if we die to the past Now.

Dying for the Ultimate Illusion

Dying to the past is a necessity; without that, one can't be in the present. Death comes always in the present, without condition, not for this or that. No bargaining at the last minute (e.g., "If I do this or the other, does my position improve?"). If you die to your past now, that makes you live in the present simply, respectfully, seriously, and you will understand love. Love and dying are the same. There is no love without dying. Love is the present.

You can't pass through the eye of the needle into the kingdom of heaven when you are loaded up with all your past and future stuff.

Dying for something, and killing others, is insanity.

Who said you can buy your way into heaven? Not with your body or any other gift to the masses like nonprofit art, billions of nonprofit this or that.

Love and death can't be understood by ego because they are out of time, formless, and ego is time, form.

Ego will have educated arguments about everything, but has no truth.

Resistance is the way of the ego; it needs war to exist. Ego creates war, kills millions of people (one hundred million in the last century), to justify its insanity.

Ego convinces people to die for a flag, the modern tea party, the pope, our lifestyle, religion, a country, an idea like the immigrants taking our jobs.

I am American, I am German, I am French, I am Russian, I am Chinese, I am Nigerian, I am Congolese, I am Israeli, I am Palestinian, I am Islander, I am American Indian; this means I am identified with a thought system, a belief that is only a thought, identification. People are killing for that and a lot less.

People have killed and will kill for jealousy, envy, competition, and lesser thoughts and emotions. A form of insanity and sickness

Eliminate all borders within yourself, and you will be at peace. This peace will translate to your family, country, world peace will not come from government! Meritorious one of the most unclean of emotions, elevating oneself above others is still believing and separation a low level of existence.

You only can be peace within; everything is ONE.

Why shoot yourself? You only can kill yourself—there is no separation! You kill another person, you kill part of your self.

Only your formless, intelligent being within you can understand.

Jesus did not say, "Nail me to the cross and your sins are forgiven!"

Jesus showed us the way of nonresistance, the way of peace.

There is no war in the kingdom of heaven; love and death are the same.

To the ego that is death, because it needs resistance to exist, and resistance is war! What you resist persists. What you fight you strengthen.

Thought, time, ego, and form are the dream of thought, living in the past or future, which is illusion.

Death is in the present detail, love is in the present detail; no bargaining about either—only simplicity in the present Now, Formless Being.

Recommended Reading

Google for more information

This is called the work, you are given much without effort nothing is possible in the work.

All books by Eckhart Tolle and Jiddu Krishnamurti

The Power of Now, Eckhart Tolle

A New Earth, Eckhart Tolle

Living and Dying, Jiddu Krishnamurti

The Book of Life, Jiddu Krishnamurti

The Secret, Ronda Byrne

Power vs. Force, David Hawkins

Power and Terror, Noam Chomsky

A People's History, Howard Zinn

Confessions of an Economic Hit Man, John Perkins

Conversations with God, Neal Donald Walsch

Modern Prophet, Edgar Cayce

Truths

Do unto others as you want to be treated

To be or not to be

Go all the way including the postage

The spiritual or occult way is also called the work

Wake up out of the dream of thought

Nothing describes God better then Silence

Don't become a seeker become present

Ask and you shall receive

What you resist persists

What you fight you strengthen

None resistance, all is one, is realization

Negativity is identification and waking sleep

The sins of fathers and mothers repeat themselves

Scientists have no problem thinking, there problem is how not to think

Love is only in the present

Killing humans by humans is insanity

None resistance is the strongest force in the Universe

Love heals all

You are peace

You are it

Stop looking for happiness on the outside it can only be found within

As you tread others so you will be treated

Be mindful of every step you take

Nothing comes from nothing

Ego is always right never has enough always wants more and will destroy itself

There is no love without death to the past.

Being is inclusive ego is exclusive

Being is formless ego is form

There is only the present Now

Being is primary ego is secondary

Belief is childish

Thought is material

You are eternity

Life Nature God is one

You can't find what you are

In the absents of that what you are not that what you are is not

Without my father in heaven I can do nothing

Acceptance—joy--- passion are aspects of conscious living

Conscious suffering destroys primary position of ego

Chastity as a means to liberation, to truth, is a denial of truth.

Die to the past

Meritoriouness one of the most of unclean of emotions

When will we act on what we know to be truth?

Exercises from the Middle Way

Living the Middle Way: Be in this world, but not of it.

I don't "mind" what is happening

This also will pass.

Is that so?

May be?

16 Gratitude and Dedication

I dedicate this book to all those authors in gratitude knowing that some readers will be guided to the spiritual path to fulfill there destiny.

I express my special gratitude to all authors helping tremendously, on my way.

Thanking my grandmother Paula that she instilled in me a sense of spirit as a child that made it possible later in life to reconnect reassemble become present to the work.